Varieties of English

Varieties of English

Teacher's Manual

Susan M. Gass and
Natalie Lefkowitz

Ann Arbor
THE UNIVERSITY OF MICHIGAN PRESS

Contents

About This Book

Welcome to *Varieties of English*! This book provides students with the study of language while simultaneously studying about language. Students will come away with an awareness of English by focusing their attention on how things are said and what uses are made of language.

This book has a twofold purpose: to teach English, and to teach it using a specific content as the basis through which language is learned. In this case, the content is language itself.

Varieties of English is an integrated textbook intended for high-intermediate to advanced ESL or EFL students. As can be seen in the specification of the objectives listed in the "To the Student" section in each chapter, the language work incorporates all skill areas (reading, writing, speaking/listening) and all areas of language (syntax, vocabulary, pronunciation, semantics, and pragmatics). These language objectives are interwoven throughout the content objectives.

Chapter 1 sets the scene for the book by looking at the context in which language is used, that is, by focusing students' attention on the simple but obvious fact of variation in language use as a function of the situation and setting in which language is being used. In chapter 2 this theme is continued with a special emphasis on vocabulary, pronunciation, and grammatical uses of language as they are affected by contextual factors. In chapters 3 and 4 the emphasis shifts to differences based on geographical origins, with chapter 3 discussing the concept more generally and chapter 4 focusing on differences in American English based on an individual's origin. In chapters 5, 6, and 7 the emphasis shifts away from an individual's use of language to more general ways in which language is used to affect a particular purpose. In chapter 5 students consider how language use may reflect sexist language and learn about ways to use language that do not reflect sexist attitudes. In chapter 6 students think about the attitudes that are conveyed by the uses of language dealt with in the book (e.g., geographical differences, sexist use of language). Finally, chapter 7 deals with a subject that is always difficult in a foreign language: humor. This chapter goes beyond the more traditional treatments of humor by including such things as language games, and euphemistic use of language.

Not all chapters will require the same amount of time. We have found it useful to ask students which chapters have the most interest for them and to then apportion the time accordingly.

Language is something that everyone has given some thought to, but a teacher does not necessarily need to have in-depth knowledge of language to use this book. The teacher's manual should provide teachers with the knowledge base needed. One teacher who taught the course, had this to say:

> I am very grateful to Dr. Gass for allowing me to use *Varieties of English.* I was hesitant at first because it had been many years since I studied this subject myself, but my fears were unfounded. The material is written so that the students discover many of the "rules" and/or concepts through activities. The student response has been overwhelming. They truly enjoy the activities and are continuously comparing what they learn to their own languages. "We don't say older person's name in my language, we say like nickname to be formal." "Before I thought Hong Kong has no dialects because it is a city. But now I think it does, probably because people coming from Mainland China before." Teaching this text was a very rewarding and fun experience.
>
> Danielle Steider

For those who may feel more comfortable doing some background reading, the following are possibilities.

An Introduction to Sociolinguistics, by Janet Holmes (New York: Longman, 1992).

The Mother Tongue: English and How it Got that Way, by Bill Bryson (London: Avon Books, 1991).

Language: Its Structure and Use, by Edward Finegan and Niko Besnier (New York: Harcourt, Brace, Jovanovich, 1989).

An Introduction to Language, by Victoria Fromkin and Robert Rodman (New York: Holt, Rinehart, Winston, 1988).

We would welcome any suggestions you have for improving this text. Any comments can be sent to Susan Gass at Michigan State University, Room One, International Center, East Lansing, MI 48824-1035, or Natalie Lefkowitz, Foreign Languages, Central Washington University, Ellensburg, WA 98926-7552.

How to Use the Teacher's Manual

In designing the teacher's manuals, we tried to accomplish two principal goals. First, we wanted to provide as much detail as possible for those teachers who are new to content-based language teaching. We would like to invite you to use as much or as little of the information provided as you feel necessary. Second, we tried to develop an easy-to-follow format that is consistent throughout the text. This format follows that of the student's book, and can be summarized as follows:

Opening Activity: This section describes the opening activity and its purpose. Each chapter opens with an illustration or an activity meant to heighten students' awareness of the topic introduced in the chapter.

Objectives for Student: This section parallels the "To the Student" section of the student's book, but outlines *both* the content and language objectives for the chapter. You have the option of sharing the language objectives with the students.

Content Heading: The content headings follow exactly as they do in the student's book. Within each content heading, there are generally three sections:

> *Techniques:* For the relevant activities, the authors will discuss the techniques or approach they have used to present the material to students. This discussion will be based on the authors' actual experience and may or may not be used as a guideline for conducting the activity in class.

Answers: Answers will be provided as well as scripts from audio/ videotapes, and student handouts when appropriate. Answers will not be provided in cases where they may vary.

Additional/Follow-up Activities: Suggestions for follow-up, supplementary, or alternative activities are provided when applicable.

Chapter 1

The Context of Language Use

Opening Activity

The purpose of this activity is to get students to think about the fact that language as we know it is unique to humans. Class discussion can center on discussions of other animal communication systems. Students can be put into groups to generate a list of three to five other animals that have unique communication systems (e.g., dogs barking, cats meowing, birds chirping). They should be asked if there is meaning and/or intentionality in these other communication systems. Why or why not?

Objectives for Students

Content

    Understand some of the ways language varies
    Understand how language depends on the relationships between individuals
    Understand different greetings and closings as they relate to different situations
    Differentiate between standard and nonstandard language

Language

    Pronunciation/perception—fast speech, intonation, emphasis
    Understanding main ideas/supporting details

Use of qualifying devices to show uncertainty
Formal/informal use of language
Finding definitions in a text

I. Speaker and Addressee

A.

Techniques

This exercise is intended to make students aware of different cues that people use to signal relationships. Before playing the tape, the teacher might want to have a class discussion about cues used (intonation, formality of language, etc.). The tape should be played a number of times to elicit different information. In question 1, students should listen only for the purposes of identifying relationships between individuals.

Answers

1. a. 1:30 A.M. Mother to a teenage child: Where have you been!!!? I have been frantic with worry.
   b. Lawyer to accused: Could you tell the court where you were on the night of February 14, 1993, between the hours of 1:00 A.M. and 3:00 A.M.?
   c. Employer to Employee: It is now 8:15. You are supposed to be at work at 8:00 sharp. Would you like to tell me why you are late?
   d. From one friend to another: I had some friends over last night. I tried to call to see if you wanted to come over. Where were you?

2. a. Where have you been!!!!? I have been frantic with worry.
   b. Could you tell the court where you were on the night of February 14, 1993, between the hours of 1:00 A.M. and 3:00 A.M.?
   c. It is now 8:15. You are supposed to be at work at 8:00 sharp. Would you like to tell me why you are late?
   d. I had some friends over last night. I tried to call to see if you wanted to come over. Where were you?

3. In (a), the intonation suggests anger/worry which in turn suggests familiarity. In (b) the intonation is matter of fact and suggests formality. In (c), the intonation and language imply anger, and in (d) the intonation is matter of fact.

Additional Activities

Following these exercises, students should be encouraged to think about the fact that stress and intonation are closely linked to the expression of emotions. Questions that could be covered include: how does this differ from individual to individual? from culture to culture? Are there instances in which students might have thought that someone was angry with them, but the speaker was only using intonation patterns that might have been different from the ones they are used to using?

After completing the exercises for emphasis and intonation, students should practice saying these sentences. This can be done in groups or as a whole class exercise.

B.

Techniques

The point of this activity is to get students to think about different uses of language. This exercise builds on the previous one in that personal relationships are considered. However, there is a new addition—that of situation.

The first set of situations should be filled in by students according to the uses of their native language. It can be done as an individual exercise (possibly as homework) or as a group activity. The teacher can then ask certain individuals for their responses.

The section in English is best done in groups. This exercise gives students the opportunity to produce the appropriate forms in different situations.

Answers

Many other possibilities exist

Situation 2:	To a close friend:	I have to get out.
	To a stranger:	Excuse me, please.
Situation 3:	To a young child:	What a pretty dress you have on!
	To a close friend:	I really like your dress.
	To an employer:	That's a lovely outfit you're wearing.
	To an employee:	I like your dress.

Additional Activities

Role playing can be useful, creating different situations/participants. Additionally, phrases such as the ones above can be written on cards. On another set of cards participants/situations can be written. Students have to find the appropriate match from other students in the class.

D.

Techniques

Before reading the passage, students can be asked to use the title to predict the kind of information they will read. They can be asked what they think a dialect is.

Answers

1. Main ideas
   1. Languages often, but not always, correspond to political boundaries
   2. Within a language there are many dialects
   3. Registers reflect the uses to which language is put
   4. Language varies depending on the relationship between speakers
2. Supporting details
   1. a. In different countries different languages are spoken
      b. In some countries more than one language is spoken
      c. Some languages are spoken in more than one country
   2. a. Dialects reflect a person's background
      b. Differences in language use depend on a speaker's ethnic background
      c. Differences in language use depend on a speaker's gender
      d. Differences in language use depend on a speaker's geographical background
   3. a. Registers depend on the situation in which language is used
      b. Registers depend on the relationship between speakers
   4. a. We speak one way to children
      b. We speak another way to adult family members
      c. We speak another way to friends
      d. We speak another way to strangers
      e. We speak another way to our doctor
      f. We speak another way to our teacher
3. Dialect is a language variety that depends on an individual's social/geographical background. Register is a language variety that depends on the use that one is making of language.
4. Answers will vary.

E.

Answers

1. Relevant words are given in italics.
   a. We can *generally* distinguish one language from another and have no difficulty stating that French and Japanese are two different languages, one spoken in France, one in Japan.
   b. For example, within a single country, such as India, many languages *may* be spoken.
   c. Within languages there are *often* ways of speaking that differentiate language users:
   d. By the way a person speaks, we *may* be able to learn a lot about that person's background.
   e. We speak one way to our children, another way to the adult members of our families, another way to a friend, another way to strangers, another way to our doctor, and *perhaps* another way to our teachers.
2. Revised
   a. We can *usually* distinguish one language from another and have no difficulty stating that French and Japanese are two different languages, one spoken in France, one in Japan.
   b. For example, within a single country, such as India, we *often find* many languages spoken.
   c. Within languages there are *frequently* ways of speaking that differentiate language users:
   d. By the way a person speaks, *it is possible* to learn a lot about that person's background.
   e. We speak one way to our children, another way to the adult members of our families, another way to a friend, another way to strangers, another way to our doctor, and *sometimes even* another way to our teachers.

Additional Activities

Almost any text is adaptable to this sort of exercise. Students can then be given an assignment to write about something that they are not sure of or that they do not want to state a definite opinion about (e.g., major scientific inventions of the twenty-first century, what their lives will be like in thirty years). They should use as many qualifying devices as possible.

F./G.

Answers

In the nonnative version, there is a definition of burglary and record, the speech rate is slower, and the syntax is simpler.

In the version to a friend (passage 2), the speech rate is faster; greater variation in intonation patterns, more colloquial vocabulary (around 6 or so); false starts.

In the version to a child (passage 3), the intonation is different, and the speech is shorter and simpler.

In the version to the boss (passage 4), there is less emotion. The intonation patterns used to express emotion are not present. More detail is present.

Additional Activities

As a homework exercise, students can tape-record native speakers speaking to them, as opposed to native speakers speaking to other native speakers. Transcripts of these tapes can then be used to discuss further register differences based on the fluency of the addressee.

II. Forms of Address, Greetings, and Closings

A.

Techniques

For this exercise, it is useful for students to work in groups. If this is a class with mixed native language backgrounds, it is helpful to mix the native languages in the groups to the extent possible. Students should write down what form of address they would use to the following people in their native language. Then they should try to determine what form of address is used in English.

Answers

Situation	English
A university professor (Ruth Sands)	Professor or Dr. Sands
A university professor (George Wilson) who is a family friend	Professor Wilson (in school) George (at home)

The head of an academic department (Roberta Baxter)	Professor or Dr. Baxter
Your best friend's friend (Roger Smith) whom you are meeting for the first time	Roger
The person who cleans the floors in your school (Peter Bishop)	Peter or Mr. Bishop
Your mother-in-law (Sally Stevens)	Mother, Mom, Sally
Your father-in-law (Gary Snyder)	Father, Dad, Gary
Your mother	Mother, Mom
Your father	Father, Dad
Your boss (Janice Bedrock)	Ms. Bedrock
Your boss's boyfriend (Peter Featherstone)	Mr. Featherstone

B.

Techniques

In the same groups continue with this exercise by having students think about what they would say in each situation. After each group has determined what is appropriate, groups can be switched so that one from each group joins to form another group and compare answers.

Answers

1. Night, night.
2. Thank you very much. It was nice to have met you.
3. Excuse me, do you have a minute? I'm having some difficulty with this problem.
4. Good-bye.
5. Excuse me, I'm looking for. . . .
6. Thank you. Good-bye.
7. Thank you. Have a nice day.

Additional Activities

This can lead to a class discussion about some of these situations that clearly differ from culture to culture. For example, in going to a professor's office, is it polite in all cultures to begin immediately with a statement of the problem? Is the "have a nice day" expression common in other countries? Does it sound sincere? insincere?

III. Standard versus Nonstandard Language

A./B.

Techniques

Activities A and B are prereading activities. The purpose of Activity A is to distinguish between standard and nonstandard language. Activity B is a prediction exercise to get the students thinking about the topic.

Answers

A.

The local speakers sound different than the broadcasters because they are not using Standard English.

B.

correct, language, descriptive, stereotype, prestige

D.

Standard use; the conjunction *or.*

E.

1. d   2. c   3. e   4. b   5. f   6. a

F.

1. A prescriptive grammar is a description of the language as it "should" be spoken. A descriptive grammar is a description of the language as it is actually spoken.
2. Answers will vary.
3. This book is more descriptive, but by including grammar rules, it is also somewhat prescriptive in nature. Most ESL textbooks are prescriptive.
4. Newsbroadcasts, religious purposes, formal letters, university activities, and political speeches.
5. Grammar: sentences that end in prepositions
   Vocabulary: isn't vs. ain't
   Pronunciation: going to vs. gonna

G.

In this example there is a nice mix of a language purist being influenced by the way a language is really being used. This speaker was arguing that gonna should not be used, yet when he actually needed to use *going to,* he was not able to follow his own purist advice and came up with *gonna.*

Additional Activities

Listen to the news broadcast played at the beginning of this section again and note any differences among the local speakers and the broadcaster in the grammar, vocabulary, and pronunciation.

Chapter 2

Registers

Opening Activity

Class discussion can focus on some of the specific language differences of the cartoon. As an additional activity, teachers can have students create their own characters where the language used is "out of place." This can be acted out in front of the class. Suggestions: an employee using very informal language to an employer; a young child using a highly sophisticated vocabulary.

Objectives for Students

Content

Understand register differences in vocabulary
Understand register differences in pronunciation
Understand register differences in grammar
Determine how differences in the formality of a situation are reflected in differences in language use

Language

Predicting language from context
Scanning
Outlining
Transition words
Punctuation for independent clauses

Synonyms

Understanding fast speech

I. What is a Register?

A.

Techniques

The purpose of this exercise is to give students the opportunity to use context for interpretation. The illegible handwriting is a way for students to have to draw on other resources to understand what is written. Before beginning, discussion can center on using what we know to predict what we cannot read/understand. This can be done with some very simple grammatical predictions (e.g., The boys . . . . running to the store. [the missing word must be some variation of "to be"]). Students should be encouraged to use their knowledge of the context (what they can read) as well as their knowledge of English grammar to figure out what they cannot read. Once students have been able to determine the "missing" elements, they should also try to determine who the postcard was from and who it was to. The type of language used as well as the content should help here. For example, in postcard 5 "Having a good time" with no pronoun and no auxiliary shows some degree of informality. In postcard 3, once students know that "I have never . . ." is part of the message, they should also know that there has to be a past participle.

Answers

Postcard 1: Written to a child
  Hi! I wish you were here. I have bought you two presents. I think you will like them. The weather has not been good. It has rained almost every day since we got here. Love, mom

Postcard 2: Written to a doctor
  I have decided to stay in Europe a few extra days and regretfully will have to cancel my appointment on Friday, June 25 at 8:00 A.M. Sincerely, Isabella Johns.

Postcard 3: Written to office colleagues
  San Francisco is a beautiful city. I have never seen anything quite like it. My stay here is too short and before long I'll be back to the old routine of work, work, work.

Postcard 4: Written to boyfriend
  I miss you so much. I'm counting the days until I'm with you again. London is beautiful but nothing looks very good when I'm not with you. I love you. xoxo Amy

2   Postcard 5: Written to girlfriend

Having a good time in Paris. Walked to the Eiffel Tower and climbed to the top. The view was great. The food's good, but very expensive. Wish you were here. Love,

B.

Techniques

Discuss scanning (searching for the main details). Students should understand that this will help their comprehension and speed of reading. Following the preceding exercise on prediction, students can be asked to read the first sentence of each paragraph. In order to make this an effective prediction exercise, students should be given a time limit to do this—depending on the level of the students, this can vary from 1 minute or less to 2 minutes. In groups (without looking at the text) they can then state what they think the passage will be about. To avoid the problem of students reading more than they should, sentences can be put on the blackboard or given to students on a separate sheet of paper.

Answers

1. Vocabulary: different words for not generous with money
2. Pronunciation: Whaja do lasnight?
3. Grammar: Wanna go?

Additional Activities

After students have read this passage, the teacher can focus on a discussion that ensures comprehension. For example, in groups, students can discuss the table and what it means. Because this table is based on the use of sentence final prepositions, an exercise or two on two-word verbs works well at this point.

D.

Answers

II. Vocabulary differences
    A. different words for someone not generous with money
    B. different contexts require different words
    C. connotative versus denotative meanings
    D. word choice reflects attitudes
III. Vocabulary and pronunciation differences

    A. formal situations—more careful pronunciation

    B. informal situations—more relaxed pronunciation

        1. greetings

        2. informal greetings are often inappropriate in formal situations

IV. Pronunciation

    A. sounds run together/blended pronunciation

    B. reductions

V. Grammar

    A. abbreviated grammar

    B. subjects of common verbs are eliminated

    C. textbook English versus spoken English

        1. prepositions at end of sentences

        2. prepositions before the object of the preposition

Answers

E.

Paragraph 1:	thus, however, for example
Paragraph 2:	looking first, therefore, on the other hand, thus
Paragraph 3:	but, however, to take a simple example, on the other hand
Paragraph 4:	we now turn, for example
Paragraph 5:	not only . . . but also,
Paragraph 6:	there are still other, one such example, rather
Paragraph 7:	we have seen, therefore

F.

Function	Sentence	Coordinating Conjunction or Conjunctive Adverb
consequence	Thus, we can think of a continuum	conjunctive adverb
contrast	however, the picture is not so simple	conjunctive adverb
exemplification	For example, we might speak differently	conjunctive adverb

restatement	In other words, words have connotative	conjunctive adverb
contrast	are often used, but this distinction is not	coordinator
choice	"Hi, how are you?" or "What's up?"	coordinator
consequence	end of the sentence, so we are not	coordinator
contrast	Rather, we are supposed to say	conjunctive adverb

G.

1. Different contexts will require different uses. These words, while expressing basically the same meaning, are not functionally equivalent.
2. Denotative meanings have to do with the literal meaning of a word; connotative meanings represent the suggestive significance of words apart from explicit meanings.
3. Not only are there instances of pronunciation and vocabulary differences, but there are also instances where the grammar is different.
4. If a person is referred to as stingy, the speaker is expressing a negative attitude; on the other hand, if a person is described as economical, the same negative connotations do not apply.
5. The language used in formal situations can sometimes be used in informal situations. However, the language of very informal situations is often inappropriate in formal situations.
6. In a survey of spoken and written texts, however, the frequency of prepositions used at the end of sentences varied according to the situations of use.

H.

The way we are using the word *grammar* differs in another way from its most common meaning. For example, the grammar includes everything speakers know about their language: the sound system (called *phonology*), the system of meanings (called *semantics*), the rules of word formation (called *morphology*), and the rules of sentence formation (called *syntax*). It also, of course, includes the vocabulary of words. Many people think of the grammar of a language as referring solely to the syntactic rules; in fact, this latter sense is what students usually mean when they talk about their class in English grammar.

Our aim is more in keeping with that stated in 1784 by the grammarian John Fell in *Essay towards an English Grammar:* "It is certainly the business of a grammarian to find out about and not to make the laws of a language."

Throughout the ages, philosophers and linguists have been divided on the question of whether there are universal properties that hold for all human languages and are unique to them. Most modern linguists find common universal properties in the grammars of all languages, and such properties may be said to constitute a universal grammar of human language.

Additional Activities

For homework students can find a text of written English and look for differences between textbook English and real language use. Sentences could be given in either a formal style or in an informal style and students could change them. Below are some examples that can be used.

> She longed for a friend in whom she could confide.
> In what country does he reside?
> For which candidate did she vote?
> To which party are you going?
> About whom were you talking?
> Through which door did he walk?
> Who is the woman you came home with?
> Look at the boy who(m) you gave the apple to.
> That's the dog that I told you about.
> Whenever I see Nina, I remember that she's the woman he gave the
>   prize to.
> That's the little girl who(m) I took the candy from.

Another possibility is to consider the following formal notice (from Geoffrey Leech and Jan Svartvik, *A Communicative Grammar of English* [London: Longman, 1975]).

> *Announcement from the librarian:*
> It has been noted with concern that the stock of books in the library has been declining alarmingly. Students are asked to remind themselves of the rules for the borrowing and return of books, and to bear in mind the

needs of other students. Penalties for overdue books will in the future be strictly enforced.

Students could be asked what makes this seem formal (e.g., vocabulary, passive usage, sentences beginning with *it,* and abstract nouns) and then to transform this into a more informal passage (example follows).

The number of books in the library has been going down. Please make sure you know the rules for borrowing, and don't forget that the library is for *everyone's* convenience. So from now on, we're going to enforce the rules strictly. *You have been warned!*

To emphasize the point of different uses of language depending on the formality of the situation or of the context of language use, students (as a class exercise or as homework) could look at the use of contractions in different styles. Below are four passages that can be used for that purpose.

Passage 1 (article from *Lansing State Journal,* July 5, 1993)

"When you're around fans and they start talking baseball, that seems to be the thing they associate with me . . . that and my reputation for being mean, or the fact that I was durable and never missed a turn," Drysdale wrote in his 1990 book "Once a Bum, Always a Dodger." "Maybe that's what I'm proudest of, that I took the ball." . . . Drysdale, inducted into the Hall of Fame in 1984, led the league in games started four times, in strikeouts three times, and innings pitched twice.

Passage 2 (from the Watergate transcripts: Meeting between the president and Dean, Oval Office, March 17, 1973; 1:25–2:10P.M.)

P: Now on the Segretti thing. I think you've just got to—Chapin, all of them have just got to take the heat. Look, you've got to admit the facts, John, and—
D: That's right.
P: And that's our—and that's that. And Kalmbach paid him. And (unintelligible) a lot of people. I just think on Segretti, no matter how bad it is. It isn't nearly as bad as people think it was. Espionage, sabotage?
D: The intent, when Segretti was hired, was nothing evil nothing vicious, nothing bad, nothing. Not espionage, not sabotage . . .

Passage 3 (from an introductory textbook, *Physical Science* by L. Nolan. Lexington: D.C. Heath and Company, 1987, p. 53)

If you go on a diet, you say you want to lose weight. That's not really what you want. What you really want is to lose mass. You would lose a lot of weight very quickly if you could leave Earth and go to the moon. The moon's gravitational pull is weaker than Earth's so your weight would be less. However, you wouldn't look any thinner. Your mass would still be the same because the amount of matter in your body didn't change. Your clothes would fit just as they did on earth where you weighed more.

Passage 4 (taken from the California Court of Appeals in the case of *Ferguson v. Writers Guild of America, West*)

Larry Ferguson appeals from a judgment of the superior court denying his petition for a writ of mandate directed to respondent Writers Guild of America, West, Inc.
Ferguson, a screenwriter, was engaged by Paramount Pictures Corporation to write a screenplay for a feature-length theatrical motion picture entitled "Beverly Hills Cop II." When the picture was completed, the Writers Guild, on April 27, 1987, determined the writing credits for the picture as follows: Screenplay by Larry Ferguson and Warren Skaaren; Story by Eddie Murphy & Robert D. Wachs.

II. Register Differences—Vocabulary

A.

Answers

Most Formal	*Neutral*	*Least Formal*
frugal	sparing	stingy
economical	thrifty	cheap
resourceful	miserly	tight
conserving		
unwasteful		

Depending on the level of proficiency of the students, a dictionary may be needed for this and the exercise below. Class discussion can focus on "educated" vocabulary and particularly on the different negative and positive connotations of these words.

B.

Before beginning the exercise, it is often useful to discuss what is meant by contextual information. The cartoon can be used as a jumping-off point. Answers will vary.

III. Register Differences—Grammar

A./B.

Answers

If students are unable to locate sentences with sentence final prepositions, the sentences suggested under "additional activities" in section IH.

IV. Regional Differences—Pronunciation

A.

Techniques

Students should listen to the tape and write down in standard orthography what they hear.

Answers

Text of Tape:

John:	Dja call 'im?
Jane:	Didn't have time. Djou?
John:	Didn't bother. Think we should?
Jane:	Could. But, we'll see 'im later.
John:	Yeah. Tell 'im then.
Jane:	Might as well.

B.

Techniques

This is best handled as a dictation with this portion of the tape being played.

Answers

1. The boys and girls were playing happily.
2. Hasn't he called or isn't he going to?
3. They want to do it now, not later.
4. He's sailing around the world in a yacht.
5. She's about to leave the house.

The tape may have to be played more times to ensure that students get all of the elisions.

C.

Answers will vary.

Chapter 3

Regional Differences

Opening Activity

The opening quotation is designed to get students to think about how the place where one is born/grows up determines to some extent how one speaks. Using context, it is possible to determine that *brogue* refers to heavily accented speech. One meaning of brogue is a heavy shoe formerly worn in Scotland and Ireland. It is possible that the dialectal meaning of brogue comes from the brogues worn by peasants.

Objectives for Students

Content

Figure out the origin of some American place names
Define dialects and idiolects
Understand how language varies depending on an individual's place of
    origin
Know two major dialect areas of English

Language

Vocabulary based on place names
Determining meaning from context
Morphology: prefixes and suffixes
Understanding features of British and American English

I. Place Names

A.

Techniques

In groups students should consider each of the three maps to determine *(a)* if the three maps represent similar areas, *(b)* what kinds of place names are represented in each map, and *(c)* who the settlers were.

Answers

> Map 1: Upper Peninsula of Michigan
> Typical place names: Ishpeming, Negaunee, Munising, Menominee, Mackinac Island, Sault Ste. Marie, Les Cheneaux Islands, St. Ignace, Marquette
> Settlers: Native American groups and French
> Map 2: New Mexico
> Typical place names: Española, Chimayo, Conchas Reservoir, Santa Rosa, Albuquerque, Madrid, Domingo
> Settlers: Spanish
> Map 3: West Virginia
> Typical place names: Chapmanville, Bandytown, Montcoal, Dry Creek, Mountain View, Ramage, Clothier
> Settlers: Early colonial settlers

B.

Techniques

Students should work in groups to match the column on the left with that on the right. Students should be encouraged to explain their choices. Depending on the level of proficiency of the students, some vocabulary work might need to be done before beginning this exercise. Alternatively, dictionaries can be used. Some answers could vary.

Answers

		Explanation
1.	Fair	This word has the sense of beautiful.
2.	Gnawbone	People were so poor that they had to gnaw on bones for food.
3.	Headache Spring	A spring is a source of water. Drinking from it in this place gives a headache.

4.	Easy Day Peak	The easy day is the resting day before climbing to the peak of the mountain.
5.	Laughing Pig	The rock probably had the appearance of a pig that was laughing.
6.	Scratchgravel	Soil that contains a lot of gravel is not fertile. The other possibility is that all one had to do was scratch the gravel on the surface to find gold.
7.	Helltown	The fact that the town represents "hell" suggests an unpleasant place.
8.	Needmore	If a place lacks many things, it needs more things.
9.	Wartrace	This is the only choice of answers in which the topic of war predominates.
10.	Whiskey	In the days of mining, whiskey was frequently consumed.

C.

Answers will vary.

    a. Named as being even drier than nearby *Dry Creek.*
    b. Often in the West used to indicate a place where water was available before the beginning of a desert or something similar.
    c. An area of burned timber.
    d. It was named because of a storm.
    e. Named because three tall pines shaded the post office on the west.

D.

Answers will vary depending on the students in the class. It is interesting when possible to form groups of students from different language backgrounds.

II. Dialects and Idiolects

Techniques

The purpose of Activity A is to get students to think about regional dialect features of their own country as a way of beginning to think about the same issues as they relate to English. It is best when possible to mix language backgrounds in groups.

Before beginning the reading it is useful to have a discussion on possible strategies used when confronted with unknown words. For example, the discussion can start by asking students what they do in their own language when confronted with a word they do not know. They should then be given a limited amount of time to locate three unknown words in the passage and to guess the meaning based on the context.

Answers

A./B./C.

Answers will vary.

D.

> idiolect—the unique features of an individual's language
> dialect—a variety of a single language that shares systematic features and that is able to be understood by speakers of all varieties of that language
> mutually intelligible—language varieties are said to be mutually intelligible when speakers of these varieties can understand one another
> systematic—regular, not random
> idiosyncracies—features that are not regular, but are unique to a given individual
> rule-of-thumb—guiding principle

E./F.

Refer to chapter 2 for information on connectors/main ideas/supporting ideas. Answers will vary.

G.

> The two words are *personality* and *ability*. Both make the words into nouns. Other examples are falsity, alacrity, paucity, sincerity, regularity, loyalty (spelling change), and security.

H.

Suffix or Prefix	Meaning	Other examples
-ly	makes an adverb	regularly, quickly, lovingly, carefully

un-	is a negative	unlawful, unsavory, uncharacteristic, unsightly
-a/ible	an adjectival ending	collectable (collectible), imaginable, sociable, understandable
-al	an adjectival ending	political, analytical, nautical, seasonal

I.

    a. disorganized
    b. inability
    c. unable
    d. insecure
    e. imperfect
    f. unprofessional
    g. unseasonal
    h. inaccessible
    i. antisocial
    j. abnormal
    k. insincere
    l. unimportant
    m. disloyal
    n. disrespectful
    o. illegal
    p. irregular
    q. impatient

J.

Noun	Adjective	Person	Verb	Adverb
organization	organized	organizer	organize	
disability	disabled	disabler	disable	
employment	employed	employer	employ	
prediction	predictable	predictor	predict	predictably
intelligence	intelligent			intelligently
difference	different		differ	differently

III. British and American English

A.

Answers

1. Four differences:
   a. spelling (color/colour)
   b. grammar (Do you have any . . . / Have you any . . .)
   c. vocabulary (elevator/lift)
   d. pronunciation (schedule)
2. Other examples:
   a. spelling: honor/honour
      enrol/enroll
      judgment/judgement
   b. morphology: singular/plural (committee is singular in American English/plural in British English)
   c. vocabulary: buggy/pram
   d. pronunciation: con**tro**versy/**con**troversy
      la**bor**atory/**lab**oratory
      al**um**inium/alu**min**um (note the spelling)

B.

clothes peg	l.	clothes pin
braces	f.	suspenders
tin	k.	can
pram	j.	baby buggy
waistcoat	n.	vest
sweets	a.	candy
boot (of car)	m.	trunk
underground	o.	subway
crisps	h.	potato chips
biscuits	e.	crackers
queue	c.	line
torch	g.	flashlight
high street	d.	main street
lorry	b.	truck
holiday	i.	vacation

C./D.

Techniques

This tape can be used in a number of ways. It can be used as a dictation; it can be used as a pronunciation exercise; it can be used for listening comprehension. In any case, students can attempt to identify (and imitate) the features that differentiate one speaker from the other. Which is easier to understand? Why?

The British speaker is first. The text is as follows. Differences should be noted in the pronunciation and/or stress of the italicized words.

The other day I took my *daughter* Mary out to dinner at the new Italian restaurant in town, and what an experience it was. First of all, we couldn't find the place. We *asked* for *directions*, but *nobody* would help us—all we got were *hostile* looks. When we finally got *there* I tried to find a place to *park* the *car*, but it was *futile*. We had to *park* several *blocks* away. Mary said that she didn't *care*—she needed the exercise and I could smoke a *cigarette* on the *walk* over. When we got there, the waitress came over and I ordered a *bottle* of *beer*, and *pasta* with *basil sauce* for both of us. As we were eating the complimentary bread, I got *butter* all over my sleeve. Then the main course arrived and it was so *hot* that I *burnt* my tongue. And to top it all off, just as we were finishing, someone at the next table knocked over a candle, started a small *fire*, and to put it out, threw a pitcher of *water* on it and consequently on me. The manager apologized for all the trouble, but I said, "No *harm* done. I'll dry." He then insisted on paying for our meal, but I told him it wasn't *necessary*. As we were leaving, I told Mary how sorry I was for the wasted evening, I know she has a very busy *schedule*. She replied that spending time with me was *better* than studying the effects of *aluminum* on coastal *bird* populations. I took that as a compliment.

Chapter 4

American Dialects

A videotape that can be used with this chapter is American Tongues. It can be obtained for rental from American Tongues, New Day Films, 853 Broadway, 1210, New York, NY 10003. (212) 477–4604. This video provides a good idea of how people in the U.S. talk. The video can be used not only with this chapter, but also with chapter 6 on attitudes.

Opening Activity

A drawl is a term generally referring to a southern accent. Students should focus on the derogatory nature of mumble and the fact that because he speaks with a southern accent no one understands him. The second quote implies that someone who has a "North Carolina drawl" cannot be intelligent. This can lead into a general discussion of accents and perceptions, focusing on similar kinds of impressions generated by speech in their own countries and by attitudes native speakers of a language might have toward nonnative speakers.

Objectives for Students

Content

Describe the basic dialect areas of American English
Know some of the differences between American English dialect areas
Understand the influences from other languages on American English
Describe how American English dialects arose

Language

Pronunciation of sounds that differentiate speakers of American
  English
Skimming
Latinate vocabulary in English
Listening comprehension
Scanning

I. American English Dialects

Techniques

Activities A., B., C., and D. are all prereading activities.

Tapescript. Parentheses indicate slight variations between speakers.

Mary (and her father) lived in a (large) white house on Park Street (with her
mother and father). One day they had a caller. It was a mangy little dog.
Mary let him sit on the rug in front of the fireplace (in which the hickory logs
were burning brightly). When she looked more closely, she saw that he was
a sorry sight. He had a sore paw, many burrs in his fur, and he didn't have
any collar. Mary washed the dog, but did not get him entirely clean. He
looked hungry so she opened a can of food and put it in a bowl with a greasy
spoon. She also gave him some water. He ate until both bowls were empty.
Just then her father came in the door. She asked if they could keep the dog
instead of turning him out of the house on such a cold day. They kept the
merry little character for many years. Mary and the dog had lots of very
good times together. (From E. Gott and R. McDavid, *Our Changing Language* [New York: McGraw-Hill, Inc., 1965]).

Answers

C.

#2 Astronomers observed a crash of a comet into Jupiter.

D.

  2. Answers will vary. A typical summary might be something like:

    This article deals with the New York accent. The accent had been
    part of the language spoken in New York by immigrants. Because of
    the greater mobility of Americans, the accent is disappearing and
    speech in New York is becoming more homogenized.

3.
a. 1. Thirty-third Street
   2. Oyster Bar
   3. Theses, thems and thoses
   4. Whatsoever
   5. Brother
   6. New York Talk
b. er > oi
   oi > er
   th > d
   er > uh (ends of words)
   or > aw
c. Irish, Italian, and Eastern Europeans
d. Those from Latin America, Caribbean, Asia
e. Police officers—since the New York dialect is a source of identification
f. Henny Youngman and Edward Koch. They probably feel this way since the dialect is spoken by lower class individuals.
g. In the suburbs
h. Bowery Dialect, Brooklynese, and New Yorkese
i. Talk to a young New Yorker these days and the first thing you may notice is that he or she doesn't talk like this any more.

Additional Activities

Some words like *Mary* and *Merry*, and *collar* and *caller* are kept distinct in some dialects, but not in others. Students can be asked to listen to these words to determine whether or not they are distinct.

If possible, you could locate native speakers in your area and collect more samples using this passage.

II. American Dialects and How They Came to Be

A.

Techniques

Students can be asked to think about vocabulary differences in their own language. Are there common objects that people from one part of the country refer to in one way, while others refer to it in another way?

Answers

B.

Examples of Latinate words are reveal, differences, language, accept-able, imposed, educated.

C.

revealing, revelation
differ, different
linguist, lingual
accept, acceptance

Additional Activities

Following the activities in chapter 3 relating to word endings, one can use some of the words in this passage as examples—the *-able* ending (accept-able, noticeable), the *-ed* ending as an adjectival form (educated), *-tion* ending (pronunciation).

D.

Techniques

This passage may have to be played a few times. It is useful to play the tape once and have students listen for the general idea. Groups can be formed for them to brainstorm about some of the main ideas and to predict what specific things might be important. The text of the tape is given here.

INFLUENCES ON AMERICAN ENGLISH

Actually, it's impossible to tell the story of American English without reference to British English. In the earliest settlement days, English settlers brought dialects from the various areas of Great Britain, and some of those influences may be among the earliest causes of differences in American English. Settlers in some parts of the colonies kept contact with the mother country and, as a result, their speech reflected changing speech patterns in England.

Trade and commerce kept open one avenue of contact, and many well-to-do colonists' children were educated in England. In spite of these contacts, one area of the newly founded colonies began to develop a variety of English rather different from that of Great Britain. The middle colonies, Pennsylvania in particular, began to develop a variety of English distinct from surrounding areas to the north and south. This difference can be accounted for in several ways: their religious difference from the Puritans to the north and the Church of England people to the south; their greater percentage of nonnative speakers of English; and their rapidly developing middle class. The variety of the middle colonies was not just distinct from its American neighbors. It resembled far less its common parent, British English. Perhaps it's not too much of an exaggeration to say that here a distinct, American English was born.

From its origin, America was to become a sanctuary for all nationalities and diverse cultures. It is not surprising that other languages influenced the new variety of English developing in America.

The Dutch contributed one of America's primarily linguistic exports, the word "Yankee." The name of the traditional fool or nincompoop in Dutch folklore is Jan Kees. Apparently the Dutch settlers in New York weren't much impressed with their English neighbors in New England and soon the name Yankee was applied to all of them. As New England sailors and salesmen traveled around the world and around this country, the name went with them, losing, at least for them, its original insulting sense. During the American Civil War, residents of the southern states used it again as an insult, applying it to all northerners. In the twentieth century it still surprises many southern Americans in foreign countries to hear themselves referred to as Yankees, since for them Yankee is a term for northerners, not Americans in general.

The Dutch also contributed names we still use for sections of New York City. Few Americans today know the original meanings of these words. The Bowery, now a section of New York City, has taken its name from a Dutch word meaning farm. The Dutch word *kil*, meaning a small stream of water, or creek, still survives in New York State place names such as the Catskill Mountains and Schuykill River.

American English also borrowed from the people who were already here, the American Indians. The names of such new trees as Hickory, Catalpa, and Pecan are Indian words. And animals which were unfamiliar to the Europeans kept Indian names: chipmunk, raccoon, skunk, opossum, and woodchuck. Also borrowed were words for things of the Indians' own construction, social organizations, and beliefs. *Teepee* and *wigwam* were borrowed for kinds of Indian housing, *totem* for a religious symbol, as well as *powwow* for a meeting and *podunk* for a small village or rural area.

The French trappers, missionaries, and explorers encountered many Indian tribes earlier than the English settlers. Indian words, through French, became part of American English. *Toboggan* is a kind of sled, *bayou*, a low wetland in many parts of the American South, *caribou*, a large elk-like animal. The French contributed their own words to American English, words such as *prairie*, a grassy flatland; *lacrosse*, a game played with a ball and sticks; *portage*, transporting a canoe and supplies overland; and *calumet*, a peace pipe.

Others contributed as well. Thousands of Africans were brought to the new world against their will to work as slaves. Modern linguists are not sure of the extensiveness of their contribution, but it is well agreed upon that such words as *cooter* for a small hard-shelled turtle, *goober* for peanuts grown in the rich soil of the American South, and such items as *banjo* for a stringed musical instrument, *boogie woogie* for music with a fast tempo, *voodoo* for mysterious rites and practices, and, of course *jazz* all are borrowed from West African languages.

American English has a number of words taken from Spanish for geographical features, such as *mesa* and *arroyo*. But, best of all, the Spanish contributed many of our widely exported cowboy words. Here are the American versions: *bronco, ranch, lasso, sombrero, chaps*, and *rodeo*, all standard words for any Hollywood western.

The list of languages that have contributed to American English is quite lengthy. It is enough to say that the language has been open to extensive borrowing, containing items from Chinese, American Indian languages, West African languages, German, Dutch, French, Yiddish, Tagalog, Polish, Italian, Hungarian, Greek, Russian, Japanese and many, many more.

In spite of this borrowing, it's important to remember that speakers of any world variety of English are in little danger of being misunderstood at basic abstract or technical levels of communication. In general, linguists are more impressed by the similarities of the varieties of English than by their differences. (From the video *Regional Dialects*, by Dennis Preston and Roger Shey)

E.

Answers

Some possibilities are:

1. a. Dutch—yankee
   b. Spanish—sombrero
   c. French—prairie
2. The Dutch name Jan Kees was known as a fool—so Jan Kees became yankee with the similar negative connotations.
3. Southerners always used the word yankee to refer to northerners in a disparaging way. Throughout the world, yankee refers to Americans in general, not just northerners.
4. Answers will vary, but in general should deal with the issues of migration patterns and in some instances isolation.

F.

Answers will vary.

III. Major American Dialect Areas

A.

Techniques

Discuss scanning (searching for important details). Give students a time limit (1 to 2 minutes) within which they need to find the number of major dialect areas in the U.S.

Answers

Four major dialect areas: Northern, North Midland, South Midland, Southern.

C.

Answers will vary.

D.

Techniques

This exercise can be used to focus on differences between spoken and written English, which are a reflection of differences between nonstandard and standard English.

Answers

This morning I *woke up* at a *quarter of nine* and saw that the shoes that I was planning to wear *needed to be fixed/needed fixing,* but I didn't have time to *wait for* the shoe repairman for (clean is a difficult word to translate; basically it marks emphasis, i.e., it was a long time that I had to wait) over half an hour while I was *standing in* line.

Additional Activities

If this course is being taught in an environment where native speakers of English are easily accessible, students can be given an assignment to find out different usages. For example, when is an object called a glass? When is it a mug? When is it a cup? This activity is most successful if students can take these objects with them. When is something a paper bag? When is it a paper sack? What is a wash rag? A wash cloth? A hero? A submarine?

Chapter 5

Language and Sexism

Opening Activity

This activity is designed to get students to think about stereotypes (doctors are generally male). Generally, it takes students a short time to realize that the doctor is a woman and that the stereotype in this case does not hold.

Objectives for Students

Content

Recognize sexist language
Understand the difference between generic and sexist terminology
Understand naming conventions
Revise sexist language

Language

Scanning
Topic sentences
Transitions
Identification of supporting arguments
Vocabulary choices referring to male/female
Avoiding sexist use in oral and written English
Using a thesaurus
Subject-verb agreement

I. Overview to Language and Sexism

A.

Techniques

As in previous chapters, students should be given a limited amount of time (probably 1–2 minutes) to scan the passage and identify three kinds of sexism.

Answers

1. Conventions of address
2. Generic terms
3. Negative terminology

Additional Activities

Because the answers to the questions can be found in the boldface type heads, it is appropriate to talk about typefaces and headings and how they can be helpful in quickly looking for information regarding the contents of a passage (see C).

C.

Techniques

In this section the focus is on having students work with topic sentences and with transition devices. It might be helpful to look at chapter 2 to refresh students' minds regarding transition devices.

Answers

Some possible answers include:

1. a. The first issue we deal with has to do with naming and address conventions.
   b. Addressing conventions are not the only way that sexism can be seen. A second way is through the use of a masculine term as a so-called neutral term.
   c. Finally, we look at linguistic degradation as an indication of sexism.
2. a. change of names, Mr. (no indication of marital status) versus Mrs., Miss.
   b. *he, man* being used to refer to all humans
   c. negative terminology (often with sexual overtones) used to refer to women

D.

Answers will vary.

E.

All entries for *woman* are gender-specific. None of the entries for *man* are gender-specific.

F.

Answers will depend on dictionaries used.

Additional Activities

Students can be asked to interview native speakers to come up with additional alternatives and to also understand whether any of these terms (or the ones they come up with) have negative connotations.

This is an excellent opportunity for students to look in other textbooks (ESL or otherwise), newspapers, magazines, etc., or to listen to television, radio, native speakers, etc., to determine the use of these devices in everyday language use.

One can also introduce the thesaurus. It should be pointed out that a thesaurus is a useful tool when writing papers since one can often find alternatives to words that are being used repeatedly. However, not all words can be used as exact synonyms. Students can be asked for the different information contained in a thesaurus versus a dictionary. If computers are available, it is useful for students to see how to work with a computerized thesaurus.

II. Naming and Address Conventions

Answers

A.

1. Mrs. Hillary Clinton, Mrs. George Bush, Mrs. Ronald Reagan.
2. The listings differ for these women in that only for Clinton is the woman's first name given.
3. It is not possible to know the other women's first names.
4. The differences exist possibly because Hillary Clinton has established an identity for herself that is separate from that of her husband.

5. Other objectionable (and hence sexist) language:
    the use of Mrs.
    the omission of Hillary Clinton's own name (Rodham)
    the use of the word "chairmen"
    the term "first lady." If a woman were president, would he be
    called the "first gentleman" or the "first man"?
6. Answers will vary.

B.

Answers will vary.

III. Masculine as a Generic Term

A.

Answers

Gender-neutral terms include: fireperson or firefighter, chair or chairperson, congressperson, crewmember, doorperson, flight attendant, poet, statesperson or politician, and guard.

B.

Answers will vary.

C.

1. It sounds strange to use woman in the generic sense.
2. Answers will vary.
3. The author is using sarcasm to make a point.
4. This would be a good activity for small group discussion.

E.

Answers

Sentence 1: I think each person should use his most careful speaking style when in the company of his boss.

Tip 1: I think each person should use his/her most careful speaking style when in the company of his/her boss.
Tip 2: I think people should use their most careful speaking styles when in the company of their bosses.

Tip 3. Everyone should use a careful speaking style when in a boss's company.

Sentence 2: If a teacher wants to teach English, she should speak perfect English.

Tip 1: If a teacher wants to teach English, s/he should speak perfect English.

Tip 2: If teachers want to teach English, they should speak perfect English.

Tip 3: Teachers who want to teach English should speak perfect English.

Additional Activity

Other sentences can be brought in with small group discussion focusing on which of these alternatives seem the "best" and why.

IV. Linguistic Degradation

A.

Techniques

As part of the issue of political correctness, a discussion generally touches on issues of offensiveness. In these examples, certain words are offensive: broad and girl. *Broad* is disrespectful, as is *girl* since it infantalizes a woman. Also, the use of "my girl" implies ownership, rather than an occupation. As rewritten, the sentences would be as follows.

We were scared that no women would be at the party.
Please call my secretary and make an appointment to meet with me.

V. Avoiding Sexist Language

Answers

A.

1. The woman who lives on the corner just got a new puppy. (a)
2. Humans have learned to control their environment. (b) (c)
3. The university's four-person crews won in both the men's and women's divisions. (b)

4. That old woman never throws out anything. (a)
5. The space shuttle was staffed by four astronauts. (b)
6. This discovery will benefit all humans. (b)
7. Peter Johnson and Beatrice Huckleby serve as chairs of the company. (b)
8. "I believe abortion is strictly a matter between patients and doctors." (c)
9. Humans, being mammals, regulate their temperatures. (b) (c)

B.

Answers will vary.

C.

1. Everyone thinks they are right. (While technically this does not have correct subject-verb agreement, this is becoming a standard way of avoiding sexist language.)
2. Has anyone remembered to bring their tickets?
3. Every student has to decide for themselves.

D.

1. Incorrect: Neither the department of agriculture nor the farmers were sure of their positions.
2. Incorrect: Each of the papers read in class was good.
3. Correct
4. Correct
5. Incorrect: Has either of the orders been sent?
6. Correct
7. Correct
8. Correct

Additional Activities

Students can be asked to do surveys to find out what terms native speakers actually use.

E.

THE ITSTORY OF OCCUPATIONS

At a particular parentent in time, perchildy years ago, hupeople parentulated the earth. In all these years, people have wondered why some people have had some occupations and other people have had others. Here is the answer. Everything was in chaos because there was no govern-peoplet. Perchildia reigned and every perchild was out for him/herself. The gendervolent ones announced that they were the perchildegers of all people. They perchilddated who would do what. Those with perchilders would be policeman; those who always childcotted goods would be shopkeepers and those who loved parent nature would be weather forecasters.

THE HISTORY OF OCCUPATIONS

At a particular moment in time, many years ago, humans populated the earth. In all these years, people have wondered why some people have had some occupations and other people have had others. Here is the answer. Everything was in chaos because there was no government. Mania reigned and every person was out for him/herself. The malevolent ones announced that they were the managers of all people. They mandated who would do what. Those with manners would be policeman, those who always boycotted goods would be shopkeepers and those who loved mother nature would be weather forecasters.

Chapter 6

Social Varieties and Language Attitudes

Opening Activity

This letter was written by a farmer to a zoo. The writer, a native speaker of English, did not know the plural of mongoose so instead of committing to "mongoose" or "mongeese," he or she circumvented the issue. This shows that in many instances even native speakers of a language are unsure of what the "correct" form is. Students can be asked to think of similar phenomena from their language and share these areas of difficulty with the class. Other common examples from English are "lay/lie," "sit/set."

Objectives for Students

Content

Understand the nature of our attitudes toward speakers of dialects/ languages other than our own

Understand some features of common American English ethnic, socio-economic, gender, and age varieties of language

Language

Differentiating between accents

Identifying the purpose in writing

Writing introductions

Combining sentences using coherence devices
Listening for specific grammatical differences

I. Attitudes

Techniques

This exercise works well as group work. It is most interesting if language backgrounds can be mixed. Students can think about it on their own (possibly with other speakers of their language) and then groups can be formed for comparison purposes. For the "other language," students can arbitrarily pick a language or the teacher can assign one. In Activity C, the students are encouraged to use their previous knowledge of transitional devices to recombine the sentences.

Answers

A./B.

Answers will vary

C.

f., a., d., b., c., e.

Language varieties arise from regional, ethnic, socioeconomic, gender, and age differences. Both favorable and unfavorable value judgments of people are made on the basis of the speech characteristics associated with these language varieties. Of course, the speech characteristics that are highly valued may differ from one society to another. For example, some people might associate intelligence with the speakers of one variety while other people would associate lack of intelligence. Though these evaluations of intelligence might be entirely wrong, they become part of the societal norm and develop into stereotypes. As a consequence, speakers who are associated with the valued way of speaking are more highly respected than those who are not. In summary, linguistic inequality produces social inequality.

Additional Activities

Interview native speakers about their opinions of the English spoken in New York, in Alabama, and in Chicago (or if being used outside of the U.S., select different locations). What attitudes do they reveal about these language varieties? Do they reveal any attitudes they might have toward the speakers of these varieties?

D.

Demonstratives, repetition of key words, and linking signals

E.

Answers will vary.

II. Ethnic, Socioeconomic, Gender, and Age Varieties

Techniques

Activity A is a prereading exercise that asks the students to judge language spoken by different social varieties as correct or incorrect. Students should be asked why they consider some sentences incorrect.

Answers

A.

All of the sentences are grammatically correct within the rules of the dialect.

B.

To convince readers that these social varieties are languages with systematic rules for grammar and pronunciation and should not be judged as wrong or right.

C.

1. Ethnic (African-American Vernacular English), socioeconomic class (New York), gender (women's use of language), and age.
2. Black English: deleting final consonants, and /r/ and /l/; the use of the be verb, and double negation.

   New York: upper class   lower class
   pronounce final /r/   drop final /r/
   -ing   -in'
   /aw/   /ɔ/
   /th/   /t/ and /d/

   Gender: women use more vocabulary choice, question intonation, hedges, emphatic modifiers and intonational emphasis, hyercorrect grammar and pronunciation, and superpolite forms.

   Age: vocabulary differences

3./4.   Answers will vary.

D.

Answers will vary. Ensure that the students have the three parts of an introduction: getting the reader's attention, letting the reader know the point of the writing, and providing background information or content.

E.

Tapescript

> V: You know like when my daughter go around, my sister's name, you know Crystal when she go around my family, they say she talk like—like she's white instead of black.
> C: Uh huh.
> V: But—what it is Bill, she talk the proper language.
> C: Oh, is she your mother?
> V: My daughter.
> C: Oh your daughter.
> V: Crystal.
> V: She speak the proper language.
> C: Oh really.
> V: And you know the rest of us speak that slang language
> C: No—Not—not like you
> C: Uh huh
> R: Yeah
> C: Why your daughter speaks proper language.
> V: Because I don't allow her to speak the slang at our house.
> C: Oh really.
> R: And plus—it comes from environment. The church
> V: Yeah, and then she in the church. In the environment.
> C: The environment uh always
> V: She—right, she was surrounded by Christians, and—you
> C: Uh huh.
> V: know the ho—the living we have, my living

Answers

> 1.   She go
>   She talk
>   She speak
>   She in the church

2. instead → stead
   the → d
   rest → res
3. In the first instance, *like* is used as a filler. In the second, it has the meaning "*as if.*"

Additional Activities

If this course is being taught in an English speaking environment, students can be asked to collect data on different uses of *like*. There are a number of possibilities. One is for students to listen for instances of the use of *like* and then make a questionnaire using those instances and asking native speakers to state what the word means in various contexts. Another possibility is to gather tape recordings and have students work out what the meanings are, possibly asking for confirmation from native speakers. Television is also a good source of language representing various social varieties.

F.

1. M
2. W
3. W
4. M
5. W
6. M
7. W
8. W
9. M
10. W
11. W
12. M
13. M
14. W
15. M
16. W

G.

1. relax
2. man
3. kiss
4. nice, great

5. both mean approximately unpopular, weird
6. dating exclusively
7. movie
8. likes, loves
9. woman; great, beautiful
10. kissing
11. apartment, house, place
12. simply a filler; yuck, how awful
13. both mean stylish, up-to-date
14. all three mean great
15. a suitor, a date

H.

Because each generation often thinks that they have invented new expressions, all answers will not agree. Many of these have been used in different generations, sometimes with the meaning slightly changed. Have the students compare the data, and try to determine the generation to which each belongs.

Chapter 7

Playing with Language

Opening Activity

In this activity (based on a simple example from pig Latin), students can work with a partner to begin to think about how people can "play" with language. Questions such as the role of language games in their country can be raised as can questions regarding other ways that people "play" with language. This should serve as a preview to the activities of this chapter.

Objectives for Students

Content

> Describe some language games in English
> Understand what euphemisms are and know how to use them
> Understand what insinuations are and know how to use them
> Understand some English puns and how to say some tongue twisters
> Describe some kinds of American humor

Language

> Pronouncing tongue twisters
> Knowledge of syllable structure
> Euphemistic vocabulary
> Idiomatic expressions
> Homophones
> Dangling modifiers

I. Language Games

A.

Techniques

If possible, this activity works best with students in groups from different language/cultural backgrounds. Before beginning this activity (unless this has come out as part of the discussion surrounding the opening activity), students can begin to think about when a secret language can be used. Are there occasions when knowledge of another language can serve as a type of "secret language"?

Answers

B.

1. Language games are games that stem from the rearrangement of sounds in words.
2. The most common use is to keep others from understanding.
3. Language games would not be used in class, at a meeting, etc.

C.

1. The general rule is that the first sound is moved to the end of the word and "ay" is added. If the first letter is a vowel, it does not move. Rather "yay" is added to the end of the word. Consonant clusters move together.
2. a. What is your name?
    b. Do you like this country?
    Students should be able to answer these questions in Pig Latin.
3. usicmay   amilyfay   ecretsay
    oolschay   importantyay   eautifulbay
    eachertay   ountrycay   andsomehay
    omesickhay   iendsfray   icenay
4. Answers will vary.

D.

1. This is called Bop Talk. My teacher is very nice. Add -op- after every consonant.
2. This is called "K Talk." Never do today what you can put off until tomorrow. Replace the initial consonants (if any) of each syllable with [k] and suffix the result to the original syllable.

E.

This listening exercise can be done as a cloze exercise with students listening to the lyrics and filling in the missing words. This can also be redone with more words being deleted. Depending on the level of the students, this part of the tape may have to be played more than once. After all of the words are understood, a form of karaoke can take place.

> Hey, everybody, wherever you are
> There's a new way of talking, and it's gonna go far,
> You take the letters in the words,
> Turn 'em all around,
> Say the last one first and you check out the sound,
> Talk *backwards*
>
> I know what you're thinking,
> That sounds *strange*
> You talked *forward* so long that it's hard to change.
> But it's just like *metric* once you get the drift,
> You *twist* your tongue and give your palate a lift,
> You take your favorite phrase,
> Read it in the *mirror,*
> Practice that about half a year
> And then *sdrawkcab gniklat mi em ta kool,*
> You're a regular talking bassackwards fool,
> *Talk* backwards.
> Talking backwards is sweeping the nation,
> Talking backwards is the new *sensation,*
> You amaze your friends when you start to *rap,*
> Don't say pass the butter, say *Rettub eht ssap.*
> *Rettub eht ssap? Rettub eht ssap.*
> And if you're out with a girl and she's a little bit shy,
> Don't say I love you, say *Uoy evol I.*
> *Uoy evol I* and I always will.
> Now see if that doesn't *take off* the chill.
> Talk backwards.
> The other day I was walking down the street,
> And there was this little girl I thought I'd like to meet.
> I said excuse me *miss* but
> *Sserd taht teg uoy did erehw .thgin ta tuo emoc*
> *srats ekil era hteet ruoy.*

And I said, Am I getting through to you yet?
She said you're a *gent* in the first degree,
And I love when you *talk backwards* to me.
Talk backwards.

You never can *tell* but one of these nights,
Those who talk backwards will demand their rights.
They'll rise up angry and get a solution
In the form of an *amendment* to the Constitution,
That guarantees them freedom of *reverse* elocution.
And every TV show that airs
Will have to be captioned for the forward *impaired.*
Talk backwards.

"Talk Backwards" written by Steve Goodman and Mike Smith. © 1985 Red Pajamas Music (ASCAP)/Big Ears Music (ASCAP)/Bird Avenue Publishing (BMI)/Administered by BUG. All rights reserved. Used by permission.

F.

Rule: Reverse the letters in the sentence.
Sentences: Look at me talking backwards.
                Pass the butter. Pass the butter?
                I love you.
                Come out at night. Where did you get that dress?
                Your teeth are like stars.

II. Euphemisms

Answers

A.

Answers will vary.

C.

This activity is best done in pairs.

urination and defecation	deafness
handicapped	death
sick	regurgitation
pregnancy	firing

being a housewife
stupidity
euthanasia
fatness
buxomness
ugliness
old age
money
blindness
burial
mental illness
failure

D.

Answers will vary.

III. Insinuations

Techniques

Activity B is a difficult activity for some students. It might be better to do all the (a) and (b) exercises first, then go back and do (c) exercises.

Answers

A.

The passive voice.

B.

1. a. teacher
    b. Students were negligent.
    c. The students haven't turned in their homework yet.
2. a. politician
    b. The other person is going to tape-record the conversation.
    c. Are you tape-recording this conversation?
3. a. investigating police officer
    b. The defendant destroyed the evidence.
    c. The defendant destroyed all the evidence.

    4. a.   spouse

         b.   The spouse didn't send out the invitations on time and no one has come to the party.

         c.   You didn't send out the invitations on time.

    5. a.   spouse

         b.   The spouse didn't pay the bills.

         c.   You haven't paid the bills yet.

    6. a.   news reporter

         b.   The police hadn't found the missing people.

         c.   The police hadn't found the missing people by that time.

C.

Answers will vary.

IV. Puns and Tongue Twisters

Techniques

In this section, there will need to be some explanation of fixed/idiomatic expressions in English. An introduction to the difficulty of understanding humor cross-culturally is also appropriate.

Answers

B.

    1. Power to the people! is a revolutionary cry. Power (in the electrical sense) is what electric companies are responsible for. (play on different meanings of the same word)

    2. Curl up and die is what someone says when they have been extremely embarrassed. Dye is what is put in hair to change color. (play on spelling)

    3. Spirits has three meanings. One is alcoholic beverages, another is "good feelings." As in "her spirits are high today"—she is feeling good today. A third has to do with one's soul.

    4. Retire can have two meanings. The first and most common is when one leaves a place of employment and stops working. The second is a play on the use of the prefix *re-* meaning again. So, it is time to buy new tires.

    5. Here the substitution is "money" for "mommy" because the rides at the park will cost money.

C.

  1. The humor in this example is due to the common double meaning of "right"—opposite of "left" and "OK."
  2.
   a. right
   b. soft
   c. old
   d. short
   e. rough
   f. odd
   g. dull
   h. take
   i. lose
   j. hard
   k. present
   l. go
   m. single
   n. back

D.

  1. The order on the tape is: 5, 7, 2, 8, 10, 9, 3, 4, 1, 6

Additional Activities

For homework students can be given the following to practice.

  Rugged yuppie baby beepers
  Cheap chopsticks chapped Chuck's lips.
  Six Swiss wristwatches
  Red letter, yellow leather
  Slippery swine slurp slimy swill
  You need unique New York
  Savvy samurai seldom steal stainless steel swords.
  Leisure lounge lizards
  Fred fried five fresh fish from Philip.
  Ike ate eight acorn cakes.
  Slippery sleet sweeps six sleeping sheep.
  Plump pesto pasta please.
  Snuggly yellow snowsuits stuffed in snuggly yellow snow boots.
  Right rear wheel well
  Literally leaving little Italy

Clark's question clearly clashed with the Queen's class.
Cheap shrimp shops seldom stock cheap chopsticks.
Full-fleshed fruit fermented fragrantly.
Throngs of tricky things threatened trendy threesomes.
Seth Smith missed Swiss myths.
Yucky little yellow lights
Charles' cook chopped cheap crispy chicken.
Shucks! Six stick shifts stuck shut.

V. Humor

Answers

A.

Answers could include ethnic groups, politicians, gender differences, current events, age differences, animals.

B.

1. Meaning: Jimmy's father was responsible for creating Jimmy.
   Revised: Please excuse Jimmy for being late.
2. Meaning: Mary was sick and I had someone shoot her (kill her).
   Revised: She was sick and I had to have her get a shot (injection).
3. Meaning: . . . and get an extra pair of ears to take home.
   Revised: Now is your chance to have your ears pierced and get an extra pair of earrings to take home.
4. Meaning: Get rid of aunts (wife of uncle)
   Revised: Get rid of ants (animals)
5. Meaning: Buy many so that you can save money. You can only buy one.
   Revised: Save money. Limit: One
6. Meaning: You will never get your money again when you put it in our bank.
   Revised: You'll never regret it.
7. Meaning: The cook has a round bottom and the cook can be beaten efficiently.
   Revised: Mixing bowl set with round bottom for efficient beating is designed to please a cook.
8. Meaning: The person who buys the gasoline must be in a glass container.

Revised: We will sell gasoline in a glass container to anyone.

9. Meaning: The women cooked their husbands and children as part of the supper.

Revised: The women invited their husbands and children to their potluck supper.

C.

It sounds like the baby drove the car into the garage.

D.

The revised sentences:

1. Hearing her name called, the girl came forward and the audience applauded loudly.
2. While he was carrying a heavy pile of books, his shoe caught on the step.
3. While we were waiting, the train left without us.
4. Having cried for two hours, we were glad to see the sad movie finally end.
5. Coming up the front yard, we noticed that the flowers looked beautiful.
6. After hearing the dog barking for five minutes, George had to let the dog in.
7. Asking one stupid question after another, Bob made his teacher soon begin to dislike him.
8. While I was walking down the path, the sun shone brightly.
9. After scratching at the door, the cat had to be let in.
10. While she was studying in the United States, her family worked in Europe.
11. While I was reading, the doorbell rang.
12. After drinking a lot of beer, she felt a feeling of happiness come over her.
13. While we were sitting on the beach, the sun was shining brightly.
14. After we had walked in the darkness for two hours, the moon rose and it became easier to see.

E.

1. This joke exemplifies a power struggle between parents and children. In this case, the daughter has the upper hand and the father does not want to lose face so he adds the phrase "at your earliest

convenience" rather than the more typical "now" or "immediately."
Again, the expected is to say "I'm going to count to 10," but he says
"fifteen hundred."

2. The teacher is saying that the way the child paints his mother is the
way she actually looks.

3. The unusualness of seeing a kangaroo is countered by the "usual-
ness" of the reply implying that the prices are too high.

4. The humor in this joke has to do with the dog's matter-of-fact retort
of being able to speak another language—that being the language of
cats.

F.

a.	1
b.	5
c.	7
d.	4
e.	2
f.	8
g.	6
h.	3

H.

Answers will vary.

Additional Activities

As part of this activity and the end of the chapter activity, students can be
asked to bring in a joke or cartoon from their own country and see if other
students understand it. If not, they can be asked to explain it.

Additional activities can be taken from newspaper comic strips: either
another matching exercise, or giving students blank cartoons and asking
them to write the dialogue.